the INCREDIBLY STRANGE 123s

the INCREDIBLY STRANGE 123s

by Tommy Bishop

The Incredibly Strange 123s

Copyright 2019 by Tommy Bishop. All rights Reserved.

Printed in the United States of America. No parts of this book may be used or reproduced in any manner whatsoever without written permission except in the case of brief quotations embodied in critical articles and reviews. For information about Muddy Ford Press, contact Muddy Ford Press, 1009 Muddy Ford Road, Chapin, SC 29036.

MuddyFordPress.com

Library of Congress Number: 2019903757
ISBN: 978-1-942081-21-0

Design: Tommy Bishop
www.TommyBishop.com

For Nura

0

Here I present you with nothing.
Not even a faint little blip.
And so you get what I gave you,
Nix, nada, zilch, zero, zip.

One lonely hermit,
    Who lives all alone,
Spends every day just
    Carving on a stone.
Why he carves the stone,
    We will never know.
When we ask to see,
    He declines to show.

2

Two lovely twins
Look exactly like each other.
But they don't look
Like their father or their mother.

A three-headed monster
    Wants an ice cream cone.
But can't pick a flavor
    From the choices shown.
She wants dirt and slime.
    He wants twigs and stone.
And the last one wants
    Bubble gum and bone.

4

Four cats make a sound that is cool,
But oh how they work up a sweat.
They bop and they blow,
You really should go,
See the kitty cat jazz quartet.

Five little starfish from Cancun,
Got stuck in a deep dark lagoon.
    They grabbed onto a creature,
    Who starred in a feature.
Its acting career ended too soon.

6

Little Jack Frost,
Up to his tricks,
Puts something new
In his cake mix.
The six snowflakes
He baked in his cake
Will give you brain freeze--
What a headache!

Seven of my lucky charms
    Sit neatly in a row:
A horse shoe, a rabbit foot,
    My little rainbow,
A clover, a locket,
    Some lint from my pocket,
And a picture of Uncle Joe.

8

Eight spider legs
Crawled up my back.
Eight spider legs
Got a swift wack.

Nine lives lived the kitten from Britain.
This was the last life he was gettin'.
The scared little cat,
Looked for a hard hat.
But could not find one he could fit in.

How many beatniks
Can you count on ten fingers?
Two artists, one poet,
Three dancers, two singers.
One plays the bongos,
The last one just lingers.

11

Eleven bunnies
Landed on the moon.
Each has a space suit
And a wooden spoon.
Scoop up moon cheese,
Shove it in their face.
Life can be cheesy,
Here in outer space.

12

Donna wants a dozen donuts,
A mix of different tastes and styles.
Jelly, sprinkled, filled, and frosted,
Custard cream will bring her smiles.
Cocoa-covered, apple fritters,
Hold the coffee — gives her jitters.

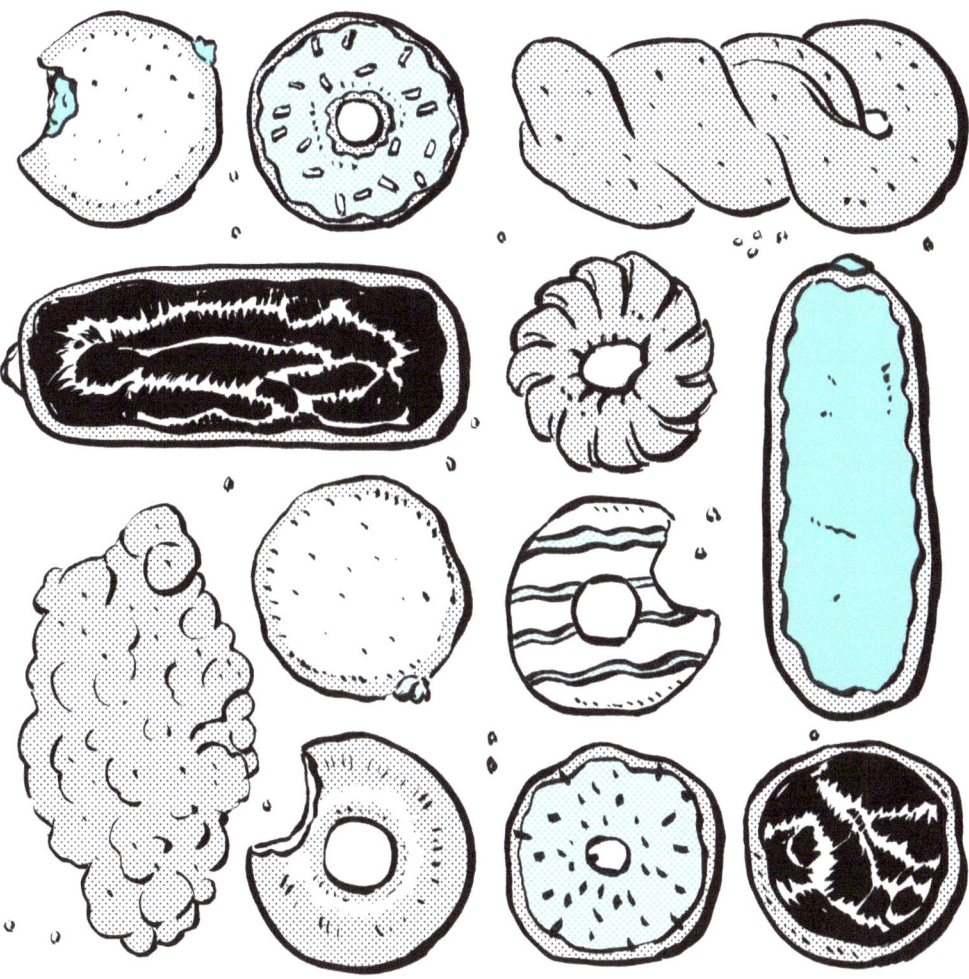

Unlucky Larry
Once slipped on a peel.
Fell through the mirror
And let out a squeal.
Now thirteen pieces
Are spread all about.
"What a mess I made!"
Larry shouted out.

14

Hidden deep within
  The evergreens,
Fourteen queens are
  Chewing jelly beans.

15

Here comes reckless Paul!
He hit too hard, the fifteen ball.
It bounced around, off of the wall.
Now Paul is banned from the pool hall.

Sixteen engines in disrepair,
From bumps and scrapes,
And wear and tear.
Our engineers will take good care,
Of each and every train repair.

There once were seventeen blue songbirds,
Who could not remember their song words.
    Since they couldn't recall,
    Any lyrics at all,
They quit and dropped on us their bird turds.

18

Morty mole dug a hole,
Eighteen to be exact.
To make a mess was his goal.
What a poor way to act.

Elda's trunk, it shakes and juts,
From the hunger in her guts.
Her favorite cuisine,
Consists of nineteen,
Perfectly roasted peanuts.

20

This bear loves sweet sweet honey.
His greed can be quite funny.
He ate twenty jars,
Now Bear's seeing stars,
Knocked out by his own gluttony.

Tommy Bishop, the author of *The Incredibly Strange 123s*, was fascinated as a child with funny books, gag gifts, and novelties. He has not mastered the art of subtle bragging on author bios.

As a father of two budding weirdos, Bishop's **The Incredibly Strange ABCs** was a revelation; far more fun than the stuffy, homogenized alphabet books I grew up with as a kid. These strange illustrations and clever wordplay never fail to illicit giggles or downright maniacal laughter from my children. The weirder, the better, and this book has it covered.

-Steve Daniels, director of *Blood Spook*

www.ingramcontent.com/pod-product-compliance
Lightning Source LLC
Chambersburg PA
CBHW051334110526
44591CB00026B/2997